Benjamin Franklin

by Martha E. H. Rustad

Consulting Editor: Gail Saunders-Smith, Ph.D.

Consultant: Alison Lewis, Assistant Manuscripts Librarian,
American Philosophical Society Library,
Philadelphia, Pennsylvania

Pebble Books

an imprint of Capstone Press
Mankato, Minnesota

Pebble Books are published by Capstone Press
151 Good Counsel Drive, P.O. Box 669, Mankato, Minnesota 56002
http://www.capstone-press.com

2 3 4 5 6 07 06 05 04 03 02

Library of Congress Cataloging-in-Publication Data
Rustad, Martha E. H. (Martha Elizabeth Hillman), 1975–
    Benjamin Franklin / by Martha E. H. Rustad.
    p. cm.—(First biographies)
    Includes bibliographical references and index.
    ISBN 0-7368-0995-3 (hardcover)
    ISBN 0-7368-9442-X (paperback)
    1. Franklin, Benjamin, 1706–1790—Juvenile literature. 2. Statesmen—United
States—Biography—Juvenile literature. 3. Scientists—United States—Biography—
Juvenile literature. 4. Printers—United States—Biography—Juvenile literature.
[1. Franklin, Benjamin, 1706–1790. 2. Statesmen. 3. Scientists. 4. Printers.] I. Title.
II. Series. III. First biographies (Mankato, Minn.)
E302.6.F8 R97 2002
973.3'092—dc21   2001000262

Summary: Simple text and photographs introduce the life of Benjamin Franklin.

Note to Parents and Teachers

The First Biographies series supports national history standards for
units on people and culture. This book describes and illustrates the
life of Benjamin Franklin. The photographs support early readers in
understanding the text. This book also introduces early readers to
subject-specific vocabulary words, which are defined in the Words
to Know section. Early readers may need assistance to read some
words and to use the Table of Contents, Words to Know, Read
More, Internet Sites, and Index/Word List sections of the book.

Table of Contents

Time Line

1706
born

Benjamin Franklin was born in 1706 in Boston. He began school at age 8. But he quit school at age 10 to work. He helped his father make candles and soap.

◀ Benjamin making candles

Time Line

1706
born

1718
works for
his brother

Benjamin did not like his job. He liked to read and write. Benjamin's brother, James, owned a printing press. Benjamin helped James print newspapers.

Benjamin printing newspapers

Poor Richard, 1733.

AN

Almanack

For the Year of Christ

1733,

Being the First after LEAP YEAR.

And makes since the Creation

	Years
By the Account of the Eastern Greeks	7241
By the Latin Church, when ☉ ent. ♈	6932
By the Computation of W.W.	5742
By the Roman Chronology	5682
By the Jewish Rabbies	5494

Wherein is contained.

The Lunations, Eclipses, Judgment of the Weather, Spring Tides, Planets Motions & mutual Aspects, Sun and Moon's Rising and Setting, Length of Days, Time of High Water, Fairs, Courts, and observable Days.

Fitted to the Latitude of Forty Degrees, and a Meridian of Five Hours West from London, but may without sensible Error, serve all the adjacent Places, even from Newfoundland to South-Carolina.

By RICHARD SAUNDERS, Philom.

PHILADELPHIA:
Printed and sold by B. FRANKLIN, at the New Printing-Office near the Market.

Time Line

1706
born

1718
works for
his brother

1726
moves to
Philadelphia

In 1726, Benjamin moved to Philadelphia. He wrote and printed a newspaper. He also wrote *Poor Richard's Almanac.* Americans enjoyed reading his newspaper and books.

Time Line

1706
born

1718
works for
his brother

1726
moves to
Philadelphia

Benjamin was interested in science. He learned that lightning is electricity. He invented the lightning rod to protect houses from lightning.

Time Line

| 1706 born | 1718 works for his brother | 1726 moves to Philadelphia | 1737 becomes postmaster of Philadelphia |

Benjamin helped his community. He planned a library and a school. He became the postmaster. He worked to improve the mail system. Many people liked Benjamin's ideas.

◀ library in Philadelphia

the American colonies

Time Line

1706
born

1718
works for
his brother

1726
moves to
Philadelphia

1737
becomes postmaster
of Philadelphia

Benjamin helped the American colonies. Great Britain once made laws for the colonies. The colonists wanted to make their own laws. Benjamin traveled to London to speak to the British government.

1766
travels to
London

Time Line

1706
born

1718
works for
his brother

1726
moves to
Philadelphia

1737
becomes postmaster
of Philadelphia

The British government would not listen. The colonists decided to fight for their freedom. In 1775, the colonists and the British started to fight the Revolutionary War.

1766
travels to
London

1775
Revolutionary
War begins

Time Line

| 1706 born | 1718 works for his brother | 1726 moves to Philadelphia | 1737 becomes postmaster of Philadelphia |

The colonists were losing the war. Benjamin asked France to help. In 1783, the colonists won the war with France's help. The colonists formed a country called the United States of America.

1766
travels to
London

1775
Revolutionary
War begins

1783
Revolutionary
War ends

19

Time Line

1706
born

1718
works for
his brother

1726
moves to
Philadelphia

1737
becomes postmaster
of Philadelphia

Benjamin helped write the Constitution in 1787. In 1790, Benjamin Franklin died. Americans remember him for the ideas, inventions, and help he gave to the United States.

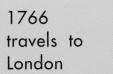

1766
travels to
London

1775
Revolutionary
War begins

1783
Revolutionary
War ends

1790
dies

Words to Know

almanac—a book published yearly that has facts on many subjects

colony—an area that is settled by people from another country and is controlled by that country

Constitution—a document that explains the system of laws and government in the United States

electricity—energy caused by moving particles

lightning—a flash of electricity in the sky during a storm

lightning rod—a long metal stick attached to the roof of a building; lightning strikes the rod instead of the building; Benjamin Franklin invented the lightning rod in the early 1750s.

postmaster—the person in charge of a post office; Benjamin Franklin became the postmaster of Philadelphia in 1737.

printing press—a large machine that prints words onto paper; the machine presses paper against a metal plate that has ink on it.

Read More

Davidson, Margaret. *The Story of Benjamin Franklin: Amazing American.* Famous Lives. Milwaukee: Gareth Stevens Publishing, 1997.

Fish, Bruce, and Becky Durost Fish. *Benjamin Franklin.* Colonial Leaders. Philadelphia: Chelsea House Publishers, 2000.

Giblin, James Cross. *The Amazing Life of Benjamin Franklin.* New York: Scholastic Press, 2000.

Internet Sites

Benjamin Franklin
http://www.incwell.com/Biographies/Franklin.html

Benjamin Franklin: Glimpses of the Man
http://www.fi.edu/franklin/rotten.html

Ben's Guide to the U.S. Government for Kids
http://bensguide.gpo.gov

The Electric Ben Franklin
http://www.ushistory.org/franklin/index.htm

Index/Word List

Word Count: 245
Early-Intervention Level: 24

Credits
Heather Kindseth, cover designer and illustrator; Linda Clavel, illustrator;
    Kimberly Danger, photo researcher

Photo Credits
Archive Photos, 4, 6, 8 (inset), 12, 18
North Wind Picture Archives, 8, 20
Photri-Microstock, 16
Stock Montage, 1, 10
University of Pennsylvania/Annenberg Library, cover